Arriving At Your Own Door

COMING TO OUR SENSES:
Healing Ourselves and the World Through Mindfulness

THE MINDFUL WAY THROUGH DEPRESSION:
Freeing Yourself from Chronic Unhappiness
(with Mark Williams, John Teasdale, and Zindel Segal)

EVERYDAY BLESSINGS:
The Inner Work of Mindful Parenting
(with Myla Kabat-Zinn)

WHEREVER YOU GO, THERE YOU ARE:
Mindfulness Meditation in Everyday Life

FULL CATASTROPHE LIVING:
*Using the Wisdom of Your Body and Mind
to Face Stress, Pain and Illness*

Arriving At Your Own Door

108 Lessons in Mindfulness

JON KABAT-ZINN

Excerpts from *Coming to Our Senses*

Compiled by Hor Tuck Loon and Jon Kabat-Zinn

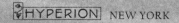 HYPERION NEW YORK

Excerpts from COMING TO OUR SENSES © 2005 Jon Kabat-Zinn, Ph.D.
ARRIVING AT YOUR OWN DOOR © 2007 Jon Kabat-Zinn, Ph.D.

Photographs by Hor Tuck Loon. © 2007 Hyperion

CREDIT AND PERMISSION
Derek Walcott, "Love after Love" from *Collected Poems 1948–1984*.
Copyright © 1986 by Derek Walcott.
Reprinted with permission of Farrar, Straus & Giroux, LLC.

"One scholar . . ." Quote # 4 from *The Heart of Buddhist Meditation*
Copyright © 1962 by Nyanaponika Thera.
Reprinted with permission of Samuel Weiser, Inc. PO Box 612 York Beach,
ME 03910 www.weiserbooks.com

ISBN: 978-1-4013-0361-7

FIRST EDITION

10 9 8 7 6 5 4

Contents

v

Acknowledgments

I am indebted to Hor Tuck Loon of Malaysia, Dharma friend who I have yet to meet, for the concept, design, and execution of this book.

I am indebted to Zareen Jaffery of Hyperion for her enthusiastic editorial embrace of this project and her conscientious and good-natured shepherding of it to completion.

And finally, I am indebted to Bob Miller of Hyperion for his initial suggestion to pursue this format, and for his friendship and collegiality over our long years of association around books, life, and love.

—Jon Kabat-Zinn
August, 2007

Preface

I often catch myself feeling that language has intrinsic limitations that frustrate my impulse to fully express my feelings, my passing thoughts and insights, in a word, my experience. Words cannot, and probably will never, replace the richness of life—no matter how articulately or artfully they are conveyed. In the past, it has been said that meditation teachers sometimes transmitted their knowledge to their students through mental telepathy to avoid misinterpretations. Exceptionally few have managed to capture the essence of their message through writing.

Jon Kabat-Zinn's *Coming to Our Senses* bears such testimony. Jon seems to be able to drop words right into our hearts, where they can resonate and reinforce our very being and well-being. Every subject that he touches upon suggests an in-depth meaning and perspective on our personal journey that we may not have felt or expressed as clearly or convincingly, even to ourselves. As one example, the use of the word "*Heartfulness*", as synonymous with mindfulness in Jon's language, can offer up new and expanded ways of understanding and experiencing peace in one's own life and in the world.

Jon's work is to be savored slowly, as in the art of tea drinking ceremony. It is to be relished in every aspect: in the here and now—as mindfulness teaches us. In moments of unhurriedness and non-judgment, freed if only briefly from the ruts of habitual thinking, the truth in his language and what it is pointing to can touch our hearts. In moments of stillness and silent introspection, the wisdom inside and underneath his words gives purpose and hope to the world.

If not for Jon's editorial oversight and discipline, this little book would have ended up with 300 longer quotes, which I religiously culled while reading *Coming to Our Senses*. I would have maintained them as they were because I felt them to be of great benefit to many. However, I am certain that when this strong distillation of the entire book arrives in your hands, your legs and your heart will invariably and uncannily, yet mindfully and eagerly, lead you to explore in depth the complete version of *Coming to Our Senses*. My utmost respect and gratitude to Jon and also Zareen Jaffery of Hyperion for their passionate work.

—HOR TUCK LOON

Arriving At Your Own Door

The time will come
when, with elation,
you will greet yourself arriving
at your own door, in your own mirror,
and each will smile at the other's welcome,

and say, sit here. Eat.
You will love again the stranger who was your self.
Give wine. Give bread. Give back your heart
to itself, to the stranger who has loved you

all your life, whom you ignored
for another, who knows you by heart.
Take down the love letters from the bookshelf,

the photographs, the desperate notes,
peel your own image from the mirror.
Sit. Feast on your life.

DEREK WALCOTT, "Love after Love"

Befriending 1

Mindfulness is moment-to-moment, non-judgmental awareness, cultivated by paying attention. Mindfulness arises naturally from living. It can be strengthened through practice. This practice is sometimes called meditation. But meditation is not what you think.

Meditation is really about paying attention, and the only way
in which we can pay attention is through our senses, all of
them, including the mind. Mindfulness is a way of
befriending ourselves and **our experience**.
Of course, our experience is vast, and includes our own body,
our mind, our heart, and the entire world.

Heartfulness 2

In Asian languages, the word for *mind* and the word for *heart* are the same word. So when we hear the word *mindfulness*, **we have to inwardly also hear heartfulness** in order to grasp it even as a concept, and especially as **a way of being**.

3 Motivations

Many people are first drawn to the practice of mindfulness because of stress or pain of one kind or another and their dissatisfaction with elements of their lives that they somehow sense might be set right through the gentle ministrations of direct observation, inquiry, and self-compassion. Stress and pain thus become potentially valuable portals and motivators through which to enter the practice.

Paying Attention 4

One scholar described mindfulness as "the unfailing master key for **knowing** the mind, and thus the starting point; the perfect tool for **shaping** the mind, and thus the focal point; and the lofty manifestation of the achieved **freedom** of the mind, and thus the culminating point." Not bad for something that basically boils down to paying attention.

5 Universal

Mindfulness has been called the *heart of Buddhist meditation*. Even so, there is nothing particularly Buddhist about attention or awareness. The essence of mindfulness is truly universal. It has more to do with the **nature of the human mind** than it does with ideology, beliefs, or culture. It has more to do with our capacity for knowing, with what is called *sentience*, than with a particular religion, philosophy, or view.

Fixed Ideas of You 6

The Buddha once said that the core message of all his teachings could be summed up in one sentence. On the off chance that that is so, it might not be a bad idea to commit that sentence to memory. You never know when it might come in handy, when it might make sense to you, even though it didn't the moment before. That sentence is: *"Nothing is to be clung to as I, me, or mine."* In other words, no attachments— especially to fixed ideas of yourself and who you are.

7 Mindfulness Is Mindfulness

When mindfulness is cultivated intentionally, it is sometimes referred to as **deliberate mindfulness**. When it is available to us spontaneously, as it tends to be more and more, the more it is cultivated intentionally, it is sometimes referred to as **effortless mindfulness**. Ultimately, however arrived at, mindfulness is mindfulness.

We take care
of the future
best by taking care
of the
present *now*.

8 Mindful or Mindless?

In any given moment, we are either practicing mindfulness or, de facto, we are practicing mindlessness. When framed this way, we might want to take more **responsibility** for how we meet the world, **inwardly** and **outwardly**, in any and every moment.

Meditation 9

Meditation is a way of being, not a technique.
Meditation is not about trying to get anywhere else.
It is about allowing yourself **to be exactly** where you are
and as you are, and the world to be exactly as it is
in this moment, as well.

10 Change the World

That doesn't mean that your aspirations to effect positive change, make things different, improve your life and the lot of the world are inappropriate. Those are all very real possibilities. Just by **sitting down** and **being still**, you can change yourself and the world. In fact, just by sitting down and being still, in a small but not insignificant way, you already have.

Get Out of
Your Own Way 11

B̲ut the paradox is that you can only change yourself
or the world if you get out of your own way for a moment,
and **give yourself over** and trust in allowing things to be
as they already are, without pursuing anything at all.

12 Nothing Needs to Happen

The astonishing thing, so counterintuitive, is that nothing else needs to happen. We can give up trying to make something special occur. In letting go of wanting something special to occur, maybe we can realize that something very special is already occurring, and is always occurring—namely, your life unfolding in each moment in awareness.

A Radical Act 13

More than anything else, I have come to see meditation as a **radical act of love**, an inward gesture of benevolence and kindness toward ourselves and toward others, a gesture of the heart that recognizes our **perfection** even in our obvious imperfection, with all our shortcomings, our wounds, our attachments, our vexations, and our persistent habits of unawareness.

14 Self-Imprisonment

Every moment in which we are caught—by desire, by an emotion, by an unexamined impulse, idea, or opinion—in a very real way, we are **instantly imprisoned** by the habitual ways in which we react—whether it is a habit of withdrawal and distancing ourselves, as in depression and sadness, or erupting and getting emotionally "hijacked" by our feelings, as when we fall headlong into anxiety or anger. Such moments are always accompanied by a contraction in both the mind and the body.

Practice Makes Perfect 15

Every time we get angry, we **get better** at being angry and reinforce the anger habit. When it is really bad, we say we see red, which means we don't see accurately what is happening at all, and so, in that moment, you could say we have "lost" our mind. Every time we become self-absorbed, we get better at becoming self-absorbed and going unconscious. Every time we get anxious, we get better at being anxious. Practice does make perfect.

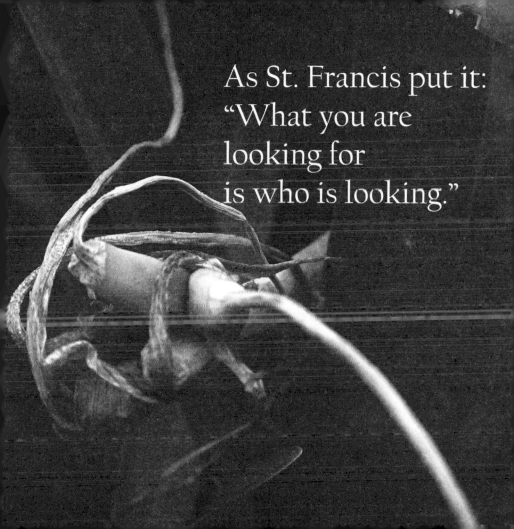

As St. Francis put it: "What you are looking for is who is looking."

Point of Contact 16

J ust as a pair of shoes protects us from stubbing our toe,
mindfulness, if applied **at the point of contact** with
any arising in the mind or body, or to any event that befalls us,
whether it is threatening or seductive, can protect us and
others from a great deal of suffering.

17 Unlived Moments

Each moment missed is a moment **unlived**. Each moment missed makes it more likely I will miss the next moment, and live through it cloaked in mindless habits of automaticity rather than living in, out of, and through awareness.

At Home 18

To be present is far from trivial. It may be the hardest work in the world. And forget about the "may be." It *is* the **hardest work** in the world—at least to **sustain** presence. And the most important. When you do fall into presence, you know it instantly, feel at home instantly. And being home, you can let loose, let go, rest in your being, rest in awareness, in presence itself, in your own good company.

19 Wholehearted

Life is surpassingly interesting, revealing, and awe-provoking when we show up for it wholeheartedly and pay attention to the particulars.

Pain 20

If you move into pure awareness in the midst of pain, even for the tiniest moment, your **relationship** with your pain is going to shift right in that very moment. It is impossible for it not to change because the gesture of holding it in awareness, even if sustained for only a second or two, already

reveals its larger dimensionality. And that shift in your
relationship with the experience gives you more degrees of
freedom in your attitude and in your actions in a given
situation, whatever it is...even if you don't know what to do.

Beyond Thought 21

Not knowing is its own kind of knowing, when the not knowing is itself **embraced in awareness**. Sounds strange, I know, but with ongoing practice, it may start making very real sense to you, viscerally, at a gut level, way deeper than thought.

Your awareness
is a very
big space
within which
to reside.

Any Moment 22

Resting in awareness in any moment involves giving ourselves over to all our senses, in touch with inner and outer landscapes as one seamless whole, and thus in touch with all of life unfolding in its fullness in any moment and in every place we might possibly find ourselves, inwardly or outwardly.

23 Transformation and Healing

Awareness may not diminish the enormity of our pain in all circumstances. It does provide a bigger basket for tenderly holding and intimately knowing our suffering in any and all circumstances, and that, it turns out, is transformative—and healing.

Autopilot 24

Paying attention is something we do so **selectively** and **haphazardly** that we often don't see what is right in front of our eyes or even hear sounds that are being carried to us through the air and are clearly entering our ears. The same can be said for our other senses as well. Perhaps you've noticed.

25 Out of Touch

It is so easy to look without seeing, listen without hearing, eat without tasting, miss the fragrance of the moist earth after a rain, even to touch others without knowing the feelings we are transmitting and receiving. In fact, we refer to these ever-so-common instances of missing what is here to be sensed or perceived, whether they involve our eyes, our ears, or our other senses, as being out of touch.

Actually Here 26

U sually, we see what we want to see, not what is
actually before our eyes. We look, but we may not
apprehend or comprehend. We may have to tune our seeing,
much as we would tune a musical instrument, to increase its
accuracy, its sensitivity, its range. The intention would be to
see things as they actually are, not as we would like them to be
or fear them to be, or only what we are socially conditioned to
see or feel.

27 Cultivating Intimacy

One way or another, our minds often obscure our capacity to see clearly. For this reason, if we wish to take hold of life fully, we will need to train ourselves to **see through** or **behind** the appearance of things. We will need to cultivate intimacy with the stream of our own thinking, which colors everything in the sensory domain, if we are to perceive our interior and exterior landscapes, including everything that happens within them, to the degree that they can be known, in their actuality, as they truly are.

Turning Toward 28

Embracing the full catastrophe of the human condition is part of waking up to our lives and living the lives that are ours to live. In part, it involves refusing to let the dis-ease and the *dukkha* (suffering, dissatisfaction), however gross or however subtle, go unnoticed and unnamed. It involves being willing to **turn toward** and **work with** whatever arises in our experience, knowing or having faith that it is workable, especially if we are willing to do a certain kind of work ourselves, the work of awareness.

It is indeed a radical act of love just to sit down and be quiet for a time by yourself.

With our cell phones and PDAs, we are now able to be in touch with anyone and everyone at any time. In the process, we run the risk of **never being in touch** with ourselves.

30 In-between Moments

What about **not connecting** with anyone in our "in-between" moments? What about realizing that there are actually no in-between moments at all? What about being in touch with who is on **this** end of the line, not the other end? What about calling ourselves up for a change, and checking in, seeing what we are up to? What about just being in touch with how **we** are feeling, even in those moments when we may be feeling numb, or overwhelmed, or bored, or disjointed, or anxious or depressed, or needing to get one more thing done?

Boundless Awareness 31

Awareness is fundamentally non-conceptual—before thinking splits experience into subject and object. It is **empty** and so can contain everything, including thought. It is **boundless**. And amazingly, it is intrinsically **knowing**.

32 Somebody or Nobody?

Who *do* we actually think we are? And *what* do we think we are? We avoid bringing our full intelligence to inquiring deeply into such matters, even though they matter most. If we think we are a *somebody*, no matter who we are, we are mistaken. And if we think we are a *nobody*, we are equally mistaken. Perhaps it is our **thinking** itself that is the problem here.

A Big Mis-take 33

We need to watch out above all for our relationship to the personal pronouns. Otherwise, we will automatically take things personally when they really aren't at all, and in the process miss, or **mis-take**, what actually is.

34 Dream Reality

We are caught believing in and living in a dream reality, invested in it emotionally, unwilling and unable to see through it because of our own personal attachment to the dream, especially if it seems a good one

Richness of Now 35

There is no time other than now. We are not, contrary to what we think, "going" anywhere. It will never be more rich in some other moment than in this one. Although we may imagine that some future moment will be more pleasant, or less, than this one, we can't really know. But whatever the future brings, it will not be what you expect, or what you think, and when it comes, it will be now too. It too will be a moment that can be very easily missed, just as easily missed as this one.

Even the briefest moment of silence is both a way of coming into the present and a way of moving on.

You've Already "Turned Out" 36

Now is already the future and it is already here. Now is the future of the previous moment just past, and the future of all those moments that were before that one. Remember back in your own life for a moment... The you you were hoping to become in the future, it is you! Right here. Right now. You are it. You don't like it? Who doesn't like it? Who is even thinking that? And who wants "you" to be better, to have turned out some other way? Is *that* you you too? Wake up! This is it. You have already turned out.

37 Every Moment Is a Branch Point

Each moment of now is what we could call a branch point. We do not know what will happen next. The present moment is pregnant with possibility and potential. If we are present in this moment, that naturally affects the quality of the next moment. If we wish to take care of the future, the only way we can do that is to recognize each moment as a branch point and to realize that how we are in relationship to it makes all the difference in how the world, and our one wild and precious life, in Mary Oliver's delicious phrase, will unfold.

Re-minding Ourselves 38

We can keep in mind and continually "re-mind" ourselves that we **can** rest in awareness with **any object of attention** whatsoever, the breath, various aspects of the body such as sensations and perceptions, with the myriad thoughts and feelings that flux through our minds, or in a vast, boundless, choiceless, open awareness beyond all doing, and be the knowing that awareness is.

39 Doing and Being

Out of that knowing, we can act appropriately
in the present moment to meet whatever
requires being met, outwardly and inwardly.
We speak of this as letting our doing
come out of being

"Awarenessing" 40

Sometimes I use awareness as a verb rather than a noun. It gives more of a sense of a process, of experience unfolding and being known. Awarenessing is a core function of our minds. While we are pretty out of shape in this area from lack of systematic attending, our awarenessing has the potential to balance out and modulate another core capacity of the mind, this one very highly developed and too often really inaccurate or incomplete—namely our thinking.

41 Taking a Stand

When we speak about formal sitting meditation, we have to understand what it *means* to sit. It doesn't just mean to be seated. It means taking your seat in and in **relationship** to the present moment. It means taking a stand in your life, sitting. That is why adopting and maintaining a posture that embodies **dignity**—whatever that means to you—is the essence of sitting meditation.

Sheer Presence 42

The embodiment of dignity inwardly and outwardly immediately reflects and radiates the sovereignty of your life, that you are who and what you are—beyond all words, concepts, and descriptions, and beyond what anybody else thinks about you, or even what *you* think about you. It is a dignity without self-assertion—not driving forward *toward* anything, nor recoiling *from* anything—a balancing in sheer presence.

Could you possibly be here,
wherever you are?

Field of Awareness 43

Once established in a sitting posture, we give ourselves over to the present moment. We can feature any part of our experience center-stage in the field of awareness, but a good place to start is with the body... and especially with the sensations of the body sitting and breathing.

44 Feeling the Breath

We are **not** thinking about the breath or the breath sensations, so much as we are **feeling the breath, riding on the waves of the breath** like a leaf on a pond, or as if we were floating on a rubber raft on some gentle waves on an ocean or a lake, *feeling* the breath sensations, moment by moment by moment.

Remembering 45

When we find that the mind has wandered away from the primary focus of our attention, as is bound to happen over and over again—whether we are featuring the breath, various body sensations, a sense of the body as a whole, or seeing, hearing, feeling, or the stream of thinking, whatever we are attending to—without judgment or condemnation, we simply note what is on our mind at the moment we **remember** the original focus of our attention, say it's the breath, for instance, and realize that we have not been in touch with it for some time.

Simply Attentive 46

We note that the realization that we are no longer with the breath is itself **awareness** and so we are already back in the present moment. Importantly, we do not have to dispel or push away, or even remember whatever it is that was preoccupying the mind the moment before. We simply allow the breath to once again resume its place as the primary object of our attention, since it has never not been here, and is as available to us in this very moment as in any other.

47 Seductive Proliferations

Watching our thoughts and feelings come and go is extremely difficult because they **proliferate** so wildly, and because, even though insubstantial and evanescent, they are so seductive.

Maybe the fear is that
we are less than
we think we are,
when the
actuality of it
is that we are
much much more.

48 Are Thoughts True?

As a rule, we are very attached to our thoughts and feelings, whatever they are, and simply relate to their content unquestioningly, as if it were the truth, hardly ever recognizing that thoughts and feelings are actually discrete events within the field of awareness, tiny and fleeting occurrences in the mind that are usually at least somewhat if not highly inaccurate and unreliable.

Self-Centered 49

Our thoughts may have a degree of relevance and accuracy at times, but often they are at least somewhat **distorted** by our self-centered and self-serving inclinations, our ambitions, our aversions, and our overriding tendency to ignore or be deluded by both.

50 Rehabilitation

The rehabilitation of the body—in the sense of fully inhabiting it and cultivating intimacy with it as it is, however it is—is a universal attribute of mindfulness practice, including mindful yoga. Since it is of limited value to speak of the body as separate from the mind, or of mind separated from body, we are inevitably talking about the **rehabilitation** of our whole being, and the realization of our wholeness moment by moment, step by step, and breath by breath, starting, as always, with where we are now.

Awareness Itself 51

It is awareness itself, rather than the objects of our
attention, that is most important. Can we rest in
awareness itself, be the awareness, the quality of our own
mind that immediately knows any movement within itself,
any appearance of a thought or feeling, an idea, an opinion,
a judgment, a longing? In awareness, each thought can be seen
and known. Its content can be seen and known for what it is.
Its emotional charge can be seen and known for what it is.

52 Soap Bubbles

nd that is all. We don't move to pursue it or suppress it, hold on to it or push it away. Each arising is merely seen and known, recognized, if you will, and thereby "touched" by awareness itself, by an instantaneous registering of it as a thought. And in that touching, in that knowing, in that seeing, the thought, like a soap bubble touched by a finger, dissipates, dissolves, evaporates instantly. As we noted before, it could be said, as the Tibetans do, that in that moment of recognition, the thought, whatever it is, self-liberates.

Waves 53

All thoughts are events—they arise and pass away in the spaciousness of the field of awareness itself, without our effort, without our intention, just as waves on the ocean rise up for a moment, then fall back into the ocean itself, losing their identity, their momentary relative self-hood, returning to their undifferentiated water nature. Awareness does all the work. We have done nothing, other than desist from feeding the thought in any way, which would only make it proliferate into another thought, another wave, another bubble.

Arriving someplace
more desirable at
some future time is
an illusion. This is it.

A Mutual Freeing 54

Through consistent practice, we come to see that we can rest in our being without getting caught so frequently by our thoughts and feelings. Our speech and our actions, even the way we are in our body and the expressions on our face, are no longer so tightly coupled to our thoughts. Because we are **seeing** more clearly from moment to moment, we can let go of more and more unwise, reactive, self-absorbed,

aggressive, or fearful impulses, even as they are letting go
of us because of our knowing. So there is a **mutual freeing**
here when we see and know that our thoughts are just
thoughts, not the truth of things, and certainly not accurate
representations of who we are. In being seen and known,
they cannot but self-liberate, and we are, in that moment,
liberated from them.

As an experiment, see if you can be here in the pure awareness of hearing. **Surrendering** over and over, again and again, to a hearing that is always happening without your having to do anything or exert yourself at all... opening to sounds and the spaces between them, and to the silence lying inside, underneath, and in between all sound.

56 Being

Practice is not about doing, or "doing it right."
It is about **being**—and being the knowing,
including the knowing of not knowing.

Wanting Some
Better Experience 57

If we cannot be gentle with and accepting of ourselves and the experiences we are having, if we are always wanting some other, better experience to convince ourselves or others that we are "making progress," or becoming a better person, then perhaps we should consider why we are practicing in the first place. Perhaps it would be wiser and more compassionate to give it up than to make it one more doing or striving.

58 Unwillingness

Otherwise we will certainly be creating a great deal of stress and pain for ourselves, and then will ultimately blame the meditation for "not working" when it might be more accurate to say that we were **unwilling** to "work with" things as we found them.

Acceptance and Compassion 59

The soil of practice requires the fertilizer of deep self-acceptance and self-compassion. Harshness and striving ultimately only engender unawareness and insensitivity, furthering fragmentation just when we have an opportunity to recognize that we are already OK, already whole.

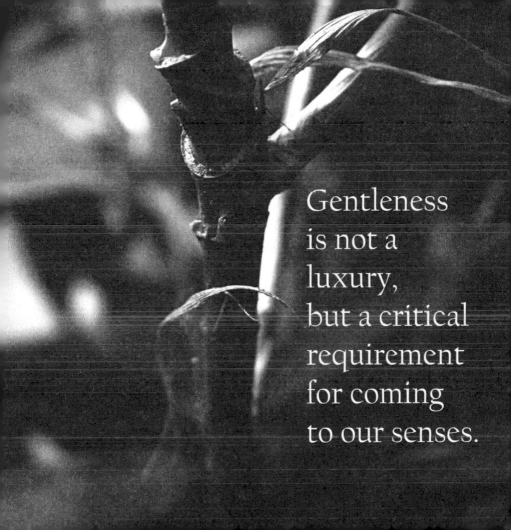

Gentleness
is not a
luxury,
but a critical
requirement
for coming
to our senses.

Obstacles Are Allies 60

Obstacles to practice are infinite. Yet all of them turn into allies when they are embraced in awareness. They can feed the practice, rather than impede it, if we recognize them for what they are and allow them to simply be part of the nowscape because, wonder of wonders, they already are.

61 Passion

The most important support for mindfulness practice comes from the quality of your motivation. No amount of outside support can substitute for a quiet but determined passion for living life, every moment of it, as if it really mattered, knowing how easy it is to miss large swaths of it to unconsciousness and automaticity and to our deep conditioning. That is why it is important to practice as if your life depended on it. It does.

Time for Yourself 62

Only if you suspect that your life does indeed depend on your practice will you have **sufficient energy** and **motivation** to wake up earlier than you normally would so you can have some uninterrupted time for yourself, a time for just being, a time outside of time—or to make a time for formal practice at some other hour of the day that works better for you; and to practice even on days when you have a lot going on and don't feel like it.

63 Informal Practice

Above all, we can allow life itself to become the
real meditation practice, so that there is a
**willingness to bring mindfulness to every
moment**, no matter what you are doing or what is going on.
Even though we call this *informal practice*, it can feel
after a while more like the practice is doing you,
than that you are doing the practice.

Teachers 64

Ultimately, you will find that if life is the real meditation practice, then **everything** and **everybody in your life** becomes your **teacher**, and every moment and occurrence is an opportunity for practice and for seeing beneath the surface appearance of things.

65 Wakefulness

Everything supports wakefulness if you are willing to let yourself be awakened by tenderly yet consistently connecting through your senses. **Everything.** But it requires a brave heart, and a mind that sees the folly in clinging... to anything.

Coming to Terms 66

Healing is a **coming to terms** with things as they are, rather than struggling to force them to be as they once were, or as we would like them to be, to feel secure or to have what we sometimes think of as our own way.

Extending the reach of our own heart lets us live in the world in ways that embody greater wisdom and compassion, lovingkindness and equanimity, and ultimately, the joy inherent in being alive.

Inhabited Body 67

It is useful to train the mind to inhabit the body, to let our experience of being alive be co-extensive with the body, enfolded into body, not as a fixed state but as a vital, moment-to-moment, constantly unfolding flow. Then the body becomes our ally and helps us to understand what we are really feeling and sensing.

68 Hearing Yourself Thinking

When at first we attempt to open to stillness and silence, it is amazing—**all there is** is hearing yourself think, and it can be louder, and more disturbing and distracting than any external noise.

Freedom 69

When unattended, our thinking runs our lives without our even knowing it. Attended with mindful awareness, we have a chance not only to know ourselves better, and see what is on our minds, but also **to hold our thoughts differently, with greater wisdom,** so they no longer rule our lives.

70 Accepting What Is

Acceptance doesn't, by any stretch of the imagination, mean passive resignation. Quite the opposite. It takes a huge amount of **fortitude** and **motivation** to accept what is—especially when you don't like it—and then work mindfully as best you possibly can with the circumstances you find yourself in, and with the resources at your disposal, to be in **wise relationship to what is**, which may mean at some point acting to mitigate, heal, redirect, or change what can be changed.

When
awareness
embraces
the
senses,
it
enlivens
them.

71 Rotation in Consciousness

When we adopt a wiser and more accurate way of seeing and knowing and accepting what is, **the dynamics of what is are already different.** Very interesting shifts tend to follow in the wake of such a rotation in consciousness.

The Unfaithful Yes 72

Saying "yes" to more things than we can actually manage
to be present for with integrity and ease of being
is in effect saying "no" to all those things and people and
places we have already said "yes" to, including, perhaps,
our own well-being.

73 Tenderness and Respect

One challenge of living mindfully is to be in touch with the natural rhythms of our own life unfolding, even if at times we feel far from them or we have lost touch with them altogether and find we have to listen afresh for those inner cadences and callings, with great tenderness and respect.

Every moment we are arriving at our own door. Every moment we could open it. In every moment, we might love again the stranger who was ourself, who knows us, as the poem says, by heart.

75 Settling into Your Body

What would it be like to **settle into your own body**, even for a few moments at the end of the day, lying in bed or just sitting around in the evening, or at the beginning of the day, before you even get out of bed?

Be Where You Are

When you are taking a shower, **check and see** if you are in the shower. You may already be in a meeting at work. Maybe the whole meeting is in the shower with you.

Awareness is immanent, and infinitely available, but it is camouflaged, like a shy forest animal.

No Place Better 77

Lying back and watching clouds, bathing in birdsong or the desert breeze, feeling the air around the body, the heat coming off canyon walls, the play of light on stone; or feeling the muscles on the back of your neck tighten as you try to find a parking place downtown in a snowstorm when you are already late for an appointment, whatever is offering itself to you in the place where you find yourself—wilderness, metropolis, or suburb, in a meeting with colleagues or by yourself—why reject where you are? Why seek elsewhere for excitation, entertainment, or distraction when life is always unfolding here and now, and there is no place better and no other time?

Without Filters 78

Directly experiencing a particular place can only happen if you manage to be present without your usual filters. Otherwise, you might only be in your concept or idea of a place, whether it be your home, your work place, or, for that matter, an exotic vacation destination. That postcard from the edge may very well apply: *"Having a great time. Wish I were here."* But you are! But you are!

79 Changing Conditions

We could say that the underlying essence, the true nature of water, is H_2O. Depending on changing conditions, water can manifest in different phase states: the frozen state, the liquid state, or as a gas. In each of these states, its properties, its outward appearance and "feel," will be different, and it will **behave differently** in the world. It is the same with the mind and the body.

Stress 80

The mind and body too can go through what feel like phase changes as conditions change. The changing conditions can create pressures of one kind or another, or alleviate them. Changing conditions can heat things up or cool things down emotionally, cognitively, somatically, spiritually. We call these various changing conditions that require us to adapt one way or another "stressors," and we refer to our experience of those changes, especially if we do not respond adaptively to them, as "stress."

Only trust.
don't the leaves flutter down
just like this?

Spaciousness 81

Sometimes, if conditions are such that we feel free from the pressures of life and things don't feel like they are heating us up to the point of boiling, or freezing us to the point of rigidity, **the mind can be quite spacious**, like a gas, expanding infinitely and subsuming whatever occurs within it, or like water, flowing freely, unimpeded over and around boulders and other obstacles in our path.

82 True Nature

If we can say that awareness itself is in some sense our true nature, then abiding in awareness can **liberate us from getting stuck** in any state of body or mind, thought or emotion, no matter how bad the circumstances may be or appear to be. But when we feel locked in the ice, for instance, we don't even believe in the possibility of water, nor do we remember that our true nature is beyond any of the forms that it can assume.

Getting Unstuck 83

O ne thing is virtually certain. We will get stuck over and over again in the short run no matter what we do or think. Getting stuck over and over again is nothing other than practice too, as long as we are willing to see it and work with it through continual letting go, and through **continual kindness** toward ourselves.

84 "Supposed to be"

The more things go "our way" for a while, the more we can believe that that is the way it is supposed to be. And when things don't go "our way," which sooner or later they will not, we can get angry, disappointed, depressed, devastated, forgetting that it was never "supposed to be" any one way at all.

Death and Life 85

Death is actually genetically programmed into life. Many of our perfectly healthy cells actually need to die for the overall organism to grow and optimize itself. This selective cell death occurs as our limbs and organ systems are developing in utero, and this dying of certain cells continues throughout our lives. In fact, it is absolutely necessary for our lives that many of our cells will die, and know when to do it. We are dying a little every day, just as we are being born a little every day.

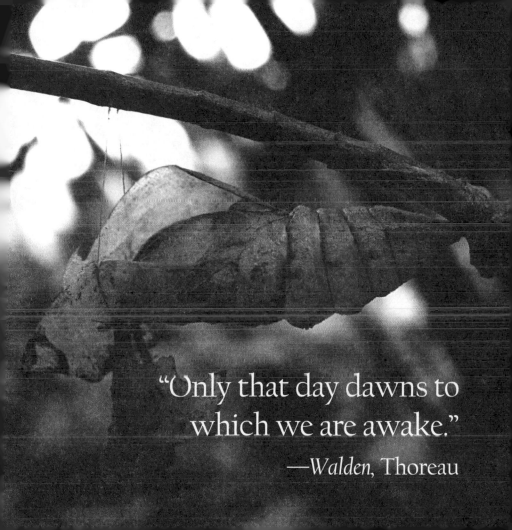

"Only that day dawns to which we are awake."

—*Walden*, Thoreau

Knowing of Death 86

At different rates, all of our cells live for a time and then die, to be replaced by new cells. This is true for our skin, for the lining of our stomach and intestines, for muscle and nerve cells, for blood cells, for our bones. There is both a coming into form and going out of form. Without the going, there can be no coming, or becoming.

Maybe even our cells are trying to tell us that death is not such
a bad thing, and nothing to be feared. Maybe our knowing of
death, our ability to foretell its inevitability yet not know the
timing of it is a goad for us to wake up to our lives, to live them
while we can, fully, passionately, wisely, lovingly, joyfully.

Timeless 87

Dying to the past, dying to the future, dying to "I," "me," and "mine," we sense the mind-essence, which is intrinsically empty of all self-concept, of all concept, of all thought, only that potential within which all thought and emotion arises. That sensing, that knowing is vibrantly alive here and, in the timelessness of this moment of now, forever.

88 Re-membering

Arriving at our own door is all in the remembering,
the re-membering, the reclaiming of that which
we already are and have too long ignored, having been carried,
seemingly, farther and farther from home, yet at the same time,
never farther than this breath and this moment.

Awake in This Now 89

The time will come, the poet affirms. Yes, the time will come, but do we want it to be on our deathbeds when we wake up to who and what we actually are, as Thoreau foresaw could so easily happen? Or can that time be this time, be right now, where we are, as we are?

For what else, ultimately,
is there for us to do?

How else, ultimately,
are we to be free?

How else, ultimately,
can we be who we already are?

Coming to Our Senses 90

The time will come, yes, but only if we give ourselves over to waking up, to coming to our senses, and cultivating the full capacity of our sorely taken-for-granted and unexamined minds and hearts. Only if we can perceive the chains of our robotic conditioning, especially our emotional conditioning, and our view of who we think we are—

peel our own image from the mirror—and in the perceiving, in seeing what is here to be seen, hearing what is here to be heard, watch the chains dissolve in the seeing, in the hearing, as we rotate back into our larger original beauty, as we greet ourself arriving at our own door, as we love again the stranger who was ourself.

Loving Ourselves 91

Can we be inclusive? Can we be compassionate? Can we be wise? These are our challenges when it comes to the outer world, as they are within the interior world of our own minds and hearts. Being reflections of each other affords infinite opportunities for shaping them both and being shaped by them. Perhaps here, too, as a society, as a nation, there is every possibility to greet ourselves arriving at our own door and to love again the stranger who was ourself.

92 Last Frontier

The last frontier for us is not the oceans, nor outer space, as interesting and enticing as they may be. The last and most important and most urgent frontier is the **human mind**. It is knowing ourselves, and most importantly, from the inside! The last frontier is our own consciousness.

Changing Lenses 93

The challenge to know ourselves is an **invitation to change lenses**, to experiment with a **rotation in consciousness** that may be as large as the world, while at the same time, as close as this moment and this breath, in this body, within this mind and this heart that you and I and all of us bring to what I am calling the nowscape.

94 Tipping Point

We are sitting atop a unique moment in history, a major tipping point. This time we are in provides singular opportunities that can be seized and made use of with every breath. There is only one way to do that. It is to embody, in our lives as they are unfolding here and now, our deepest values and our understanding of what is most important—and share it with each other, trusting that such embodied actions, on even the smallest of scales, will entrain the world over time into greater wisdom and health and sanity.

Simply bearing witness
changes everything.

95 Bearing Witness

Gandhi knew that. Martin Luther King knew that. Joan of Arc knew that. All three **moved mountains with their conviction**, and all three paid for it with their lives, which only served to move the mountains even further. They stood for and behind what they knew 100 percent. And they knew it from the heart at least as much as from their heads. There is nothing passive about taking a stand in this way.

The World Will Shift 96

Y ou don't necessarily have to surrender your life to bear witness to injustice and suffering. The more bearing witness while **dwelling in openhearted awareness** becomes a way of life for all of us, the more the world will shift, because the world itself is none other than us. But it is

sometimes, more often than not, a long, slow process,
the work of generations. And yet, at times, a tipping point is
reached that could not be predicted even one moment before. And
then things shift, rotate, transform
and very quickly.

No Absolutes 97

The more we say or think that we absolutely know what is right, the more likely we are to believe it. It becomes another **unexamined construct** of the mind, and thus an **impediment** to the very freedom and honesty and true morality we are advocating for others and claiming we live by and enjoy. You can just feel how dangerous that kind of thinking is, especially if we are unaware of it, because that is just what everybody feels, no matter what side of an issue they fall on. "I am right and they are wrong." "I know what is right, and they don't." "What is wrong with them?" Then we start attributing motive. Right away, we're in trouble.

Mutual Understanding

98

Mindful dialogue invites true listening, and true listening expands our ways of knowing and understanding. Ultimately, it elevates discourse, and makes it more likely that we will gradually **learn and grow** from understanding one another's perspectives rather than just fortifying our positions and stereotyping all those who disagree with us.

99 Liberation

Mindfulness is really about freedom. It is first and foremost a **liberative practice**. It is a way of being that gives us back our life, and our happiness, right here, right now—that wrests it from the jaws of unawareness and habits of inattention and somnambulance that threaten to **imprison** us in ways that can be as painful, ultimately, as losing our outward freedoms. And one way it frees us is from continually making the same unwise decisions when the consequences of such are staring us right in the face and could be apprehended, if only we would **look** and **actually see**.

Democracy 100

Mindfulness can be a natural catalyst in deepening and broadening democracy, a democracy in which liberty is embodied not only in our rhetoric and in our laws and institutions, and how they are implemented in practice—as important as that is—but also in our **hard-earned wisdom** and **compassion** as individual citizens. Peace and happiness are not commodities to be acquired or conferred but qualities that are **embodied** and **lived**. They can only be embodied and lived in practice, not merely in the enunciation of principles, however lofty.

"The true journey of discovery consists not in seeking new landscapes but in having fresh eyes."

—Marcel Proust

Unhealthy World 101

If others are not free, then in a very real way, we **cannot** be completely free or at peace either, just as we cannot be completely healthy in an unhealthy world.

102 Suspension of Distraction

Perhaps it is time to make the suspension of distraction a way of life. Imagine how healthy it might be for us personally, and for the world at large. We might truly come to know peace because we would be peaceful. Not naïve, not weak, not powerless, but truly powerful, peace-embodying and peace-appreciating, in our true strength, in our true wisdom.

Silence Is Prayer 103

When a loss stirs great sadness and grief in us, after the wailing and the tears and the tearing of our hair, there comes a time when we have to fall silent. Silence is the ultimate prayer.

104 Observance

We call a moment of silence an **observance**. How appropriate. It is a moment of pure being. It is also a nod to something deep within ourselves that we touch only briefly and then shy away from, perhaps out of discomfort or pure unfamiliarity. It is a **bearing witness**. In that bearing witness, we not only bear our burden better, but we demonstrate that we are larger than it is, that we have the capacity to hold it, to honor it, and to make a context for it and for ourselves, and so grow beyond it without ever forgetting.

Wake-up Call 105

The bell of mindfulness **tolls in each moment,** inviting us to **come to our senses**, reminding us that we can wake up to our lives, now, while we have them to live.

106 Interconnectedness

We humans are all intimately interconnected. How we treat each other matters to the health and well-being, perhaps even the survival, of us all as a species, not in some vague future, but in this very moment. Kindness is the natural response to recognizing interconnectedness. And in that kindness is true wisdom.

Owning What We Call Ourselves

Perhaps it is time for us to own the name we have given ourselves as a species, *Homo sapiens sapiens—the species that knows and knows that it knows*—to own our sentience and literally and metaphorically **come to our senses** while there is still time.

108 All Else Will Follow

What is at stake, finally, is none other than our very hearts, our very humanity, our species, and our world. What is available to us is the full spectrum of who and what we are. What is required is nothing special, simply that we start **paying attention** and **wake up to things as they are.** All else will follow.

ARRIVING AT YOUR OWN DOOR